Karate FOR Kids

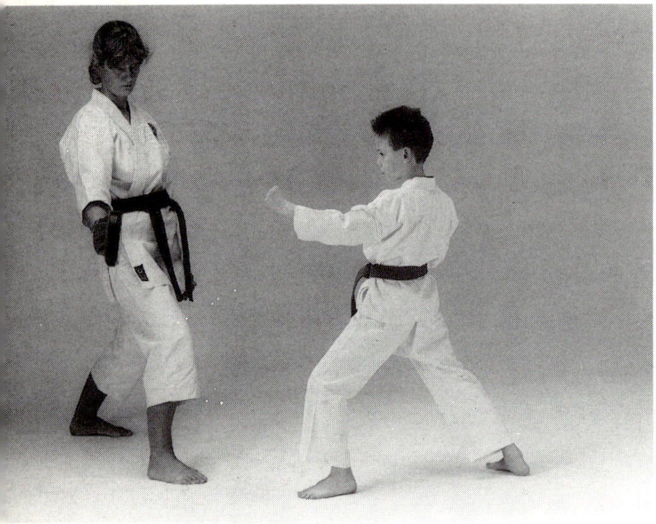

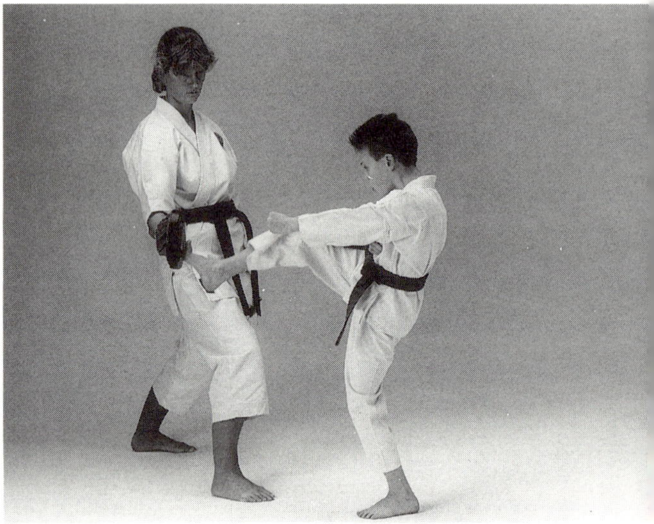

Karate FOR Kids

VINCE MORRIS
AND
AIDAN TRIMBLE

STANLEY PAUL
LONDON · SYDNEY · AUCKLAND · JOHANNESBURG

By the same authors:
Advanced Karate Manual (Stanley Paul, 1989)
Karate Kata and Applications 1–4 (Stanley Paul, 1990/1)
The Karate-Dō Manual, by Vince Morris (Stanley Paul, 1979)

Stanley Paul & Co. Ltd
An imprint of Random Century Group

20 Vauxhall Bridge Road, London SW1V 2SA

Random Century Australia (Pty) Ltd
20 Alfred Street, Milsons Point, Sydney 2061

Random Century New Zealand Limited
PO Box 40-086, Glenfield, Auckland 10

Century Hutchinson South Africa (Pty) Ltd
PO Box 337, Bergvlei 2012, South Africa

First published 1991
Copyright © Vince Morris and Aidan Trimble, 1991

The right of Vince Morris and Aidan Trimble to be identified as the authors of this work has been asserted by them in accordance with the Copyright, Designs and Patents Act, 1988

All rights reserved
Set in 11/13pt Berkeley Old Style Book by SX Composing Ltd, Rayleigh, Essex.
Printed and bound in Great Britain by Clays Ltd, St Ives plc.
A catalogue record for this book is available from the British Library

ISBN 0 09 174590 X

Vince
For my two sons, Gareth and Adrian

Aidan
For my mother and father, Maureen and Michael

Contents

ACKNOWLEDGEMENTS	8
QUESTIONS TO THE MASTER	10
TYPES OF ACTIVITIES	27
WARM-UP AND STRETCHING EXERCISES	27
CROSS-TRAINING EXERCISES	37
SELF-DEFENCE	41
TECHNIQUES	43
DISALLOWED TECHNIQUES	43
BREAKFALL TECHNIQUES	43
STANCES	43
BLOCKS	44
PUNCHES	50
KICKS	56
SOLO PRACTICE	68
PARTNER WORK AND SPARRING	68
KATA	84

COMPETITION	86
THE COMPETITION RULES AND AREA	88
TAKING PART IN A COMPETITION	89

THE TIGER CLUB AND NEWSLETTER	93
YOU HAVE A RIGHT TO PROTECT YOURSELF!	93
ADVICE TO TEENAGERS	94
GLOSSARY	96

Acknowledgements

Aidan and Vince would like to thank Neil Sutcliffe and Debbie Beevers, Adam Fewkes, David Rose, Mya Foster, Nick Allen and Jodi Steptoe for their help in posing for the photographs.

Our thanks are also due to Noel McCarthy and Bob Hayes for the photography.

Naturally, none of this would have been possible without the encouragement of Roddy Bloomfield and Dominique Shead at Century Hutchinson.

Left: Vince Morris
Above: Aidan Trimble

Notes to Parents and Coaches

It is important to remember that young boys and girls will not have the same co-ordination or strength as adults, nor will they have the same ability to concentrate for more than short periods of time.

Because of the underdeveloped nature of muscles and joints, it would be all too easy to permanently damage a young person's body by trying to get them to train in the same way as grown-ups.

It is also very important that the *Sensei* realises that because of the lack of what is called "fast-twitch" muscle fibre before the onset of puberty (the sort that is most utilised in explosive-type short-burst activity) young students are best suited to low-intensity endurance (aerobic) type exercise, rather than to periods of high intensity (anaerobic) exercise, which will require long rest periods to allow the body time to deal with the waste products which will be formed from the muscle activity.

Questions to the Master

Q Master, why do we call you "**Sensei**"?

A It simply means "Teacher", and it is Japanese because that is the world-wide language of Karate, just as English is for cricket and boxing, and French is for fencing. This means that you can go anywhere in the world and still be able to continue with your practice.

Q What does "Karate" mean?

A Literally it means "empty hand(s)", signifying that it is an effective system of self-defence using primarily only the body's natural weapons. It also has a more subtle meaning, implying that the user is empty of self-interest and is able to view situations clearly and with wisdom.

Q How and when did Karate start?

A There are records of various fighting methods dating back many, many centuries (over 3,000 years, in fact), and the origins of Karate itself are hidden in the distant past, but tradition has it that over a 1,000 years ago there lived in China a wise Buddhist priest by the name of

Questions to the Master

Bodhidharma who devised a system of exercises to help his fellow monks become stronger and better able to meditate.

It seems that these exercises were based upon yoga-like stretching and breathing routines and were developed into a system of self-defence which eventually became known as *Shorinji-Kempo* (Shaolin-Kempo in Chinese) deriving from the name of the Temple where the monks were taught. China in those days was a pretty lawless place, and it was necessary – even for a monk – to be able to defend oneself against attack by bandits.

Later, in the course of history, trade between China and the island of Okinawa developed, and some elements of the Chinese fighting systems were introduced into those of the native Okinawans. From this mixture a number of slightly differing systems emerged, known overall as *Okinawa-te* (Okinawa-hand(s)) or *Tang-te* (Chinese-hand(s)).

In 1922 an Okinawan expert called Gichin Funakoshi went to Japan to demonstrate his particular style and was so well received that he settled and began to teach. He it was who changed the name of the fighting system from "Chinese-hand(s)" to that of "empty hand(s)" which it has today. After many hard years he founded the most successful style of Karate, which was called *Shotokan* by his followers, *Shoto* being a pen-name of Funakoshi's and *kan*

Questions to the Master

meaning "hall" or "meeting place".

Since then other styles have developed and grown in number, but *Shotokan* remains the most popular and widely practised throughout the world. Some of the other styles which you may find being practised are: *Wado-ryu, Kyokushinkai, Ishin-ryu, Goju-ryu,* and *Shito-ryu*. There is also a Korean form of Karate called *Taikwondo*.

Q Do I have to go to Japan to get the best instruction?

A No. Although there are of course good teachers in Japan, many of the best left to spread the art throughout the world, and indeed many of their students have surpassed their masters and are more able to teach in a scientific and safe way, more suited to the Western method of doing things, rather than in the rather more severe Japanese way.

Q Master, what is meditation, and do I need to do it to be good at Karate?

A Well, that really all depends on what you mean by "good at Karate". To begin with, meditation is nothing to do with religion, although it is often used by religious people. Basically it is a way of quietening the mind, so as to see into the truth of things. It is possible to be good at any technique in Karate without meditating at all! On the other hand, to gain strength of body you have to continually exercise the body; don't you think, then, that it follows that to gain strength of mind you will have to exercise the mind?

The Japanese *Samurai* warriors used meditation techniques to help them to overcome fear and thus become better fighters, so to dismiss meditation out of hand would perhaps be a little foolish.

Formal bow and meditation posture:

Heisoku-dachi

Questions to the Master

Q Master, how do I meditate, and does it take a long time?

A Well, to begin with all you need do is go to a quiet spot for just ten minutes every day, and sit cross-legged on a cushion where you will not be disturbed. Just close your eyes, sit up straight, and simply let all your tension go. In your mind, watch yourself breathing in and out, and try to count your breaths each time that you breathe in. Don't try to control your breathing, just count to ten, and start again. It sounds easy, but I warn you it is not!

Another old technique to calm the mind is to imagine, as you sit, that you can see a lighted candle in front of you. Concentrate on the flickering candle-flame, cutting out all other thoughts. When you can do this every time successfully you will be starting to have control, and then, when you feel stressed or worried you can ease the tension by quietly practising your breathing techniques.

Of course, there is more to it than that, but you will need a good teacher to get you further, and this will be a good start.

Q Master, is this what we should be doing when we kneel down at the end of each training session?

A Ah! You are talking about *Mokuso*. Well, there are a number of reasons for this quiet period, and in a sense it is a type of meditation. Briefly, you should try to sit with your back straight and your shoulders back, not slumped.

If your training session has finished you should allow your breathing to get back to normal after the exertions of the training. Now, your mind can be doing various things to return you to a calm state, as in ordinary meditation. You could be just

Knees out, back straight

14 Questions to the Master

Right: Left knee down

Far right: Both knees down

Below right: Eyes closed, upright posture

Below far right: Left hand down

Bottom right: Both hands down

Bottom far right: Bow

counting your breaths and watching as they become quieter. Or you could be saying to yourself that with every in-breath you are feeling stronger and more relaxed. You should soon be feeling calm and full of energy.

If, on the other hand, *Mokuso* is either before or during the session, you should be quietly concentrating your mind on trying your utmost to train hard and to master the essence of whatever technique or skill is to be practised.

Questions to the Master

Q Master, talking of breathing, I tend to get asthma when I train. Should I still practise?

A Oh yes, most certainly! In fact, as long as you make sure that whoever is taking the class knows that you suffer from asthma, and as long as you are sensible and rest when you feel an attack coming on, then your training will do you good. Quite a number of excellent football players, swimmers, athletes and *Karate-ka* have used their discipline to help them improve their fitness and control their illness.

Of course, I am not just talking about breathing difficulties. Very many types of physical disability in young students can be helped by Karate training. I repeat, however, that you should always make sure that the *Sensei* knows of your problem.

Q Why do I need to wear a special suit?

A Well, you don't really. Karate can be practised in a track-suit, in ordinary clothes, or whatever, but the wearing of a white cotton **Gi** as it is called, is traditional, and is also functional, being strengthened to be able to cope with the rough and tumble of fighting. In some styles a coloured *Gi* is worn, but for the majority of the Karate styles the colour is white.

Questions to the Master

Q Why are there different coloured belts?

A Practically all Karate styles use a coloured belt system to denote the skill-level of the wearer. Generally there is a three-month gap between gradings for the **Kyu** grades (those beneath Black Belt). The gap between **Dan** gradings (Black Belt) is much longer, often a matter of years for the higher grades.

Q Why do we bow as we enter the practice hall and when we meet another teacher or student?

A The bow, or **Rei** in Japanese, is a sign of respectful greeting, much as the handshake is in the West, but it also carries the idea of respect for the efforts of others on the Way of Karate.

Of course, it can be just a meaningless gesture, a quick bob of the head, but it shouldn't be. When you enter the **Dojo** the bow should remind you of the serious nature of your training and of your commitment to it. (But don't think that you shouldn't enjoy your Karate. It should be fun, and you should look forward to your training; but you do have to remember that it is a combat art, and you must always take care not to hurt your partner.)

Remember that when you bow you should not rush it, and it is generally considered to be bad-mannered to look directly at the face of the person to whom you are bowing; you should look at the centre of the body.

Questions to the Master | 17

Bow-rei: (left to right) Heisoku-dachi, Musubi-dachi rei, Musubi-dachi

Q Is it the same when you do a kneeling bow? Why do we have to lower the left knee first?

A Yes. It is just the same, and the reason for always kneeling with the left knee first is traditional, stemming from the days when the *Samurai* used to wear the *Dai-Sho*, the two swords, which were worn through the *Obi* (belt) on the left-hand side, so that they were drawn with the right hand. If you think about it, kneeling with the right knee first makes it more difficult to draw a sword to defend yourself with in the event of a surprise attack.

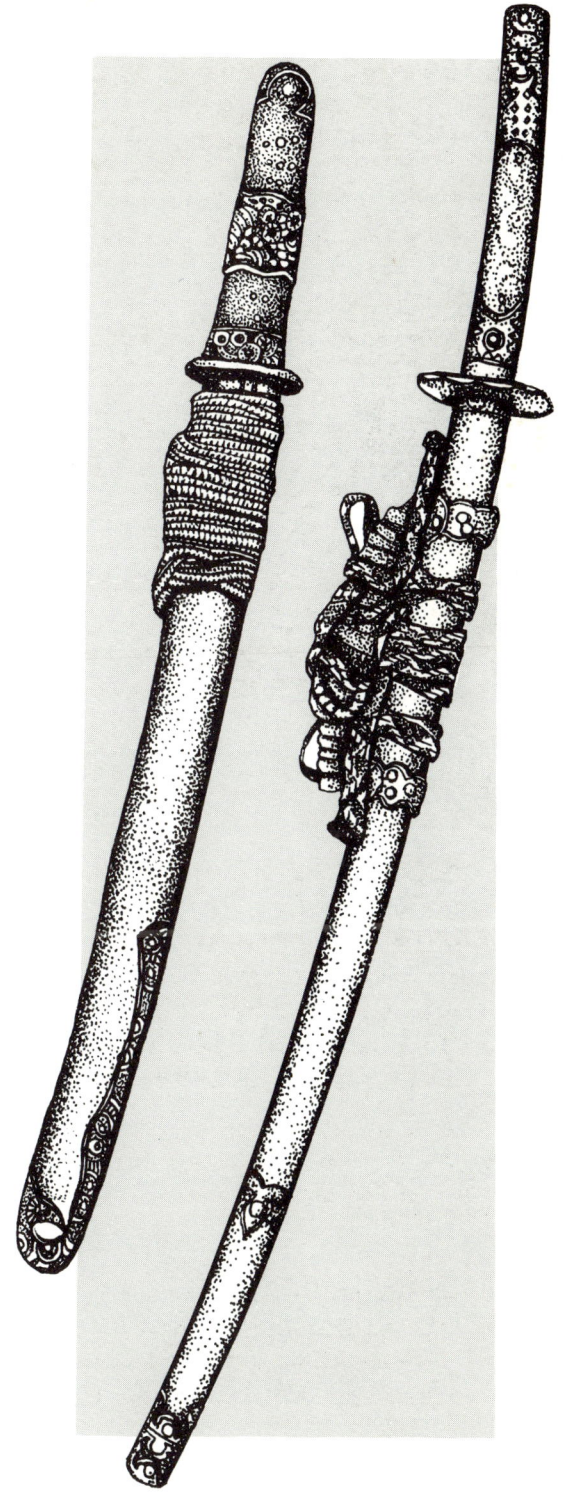

18 Questions to the Master

Q Master, I keep hearing people saying "Uss" or "Oss" when they meet. What does it mean?

A "Oss" is a special salutation in the Martial Arts, and particularly in Karate, and it can mean many things, from a simple greeting to a friend, to being a sign of determination before you start practising any particular technique.

Q Teacher, why do we have to shout when we do a technique? It makes me feel a little bit silly!

A Aha! The **Kiai**! Well, there are a number of reasons, and as it is important for you to understand I will try to explain briefly.

In Japanese it is a combination of words meaning "spirit" and "meeting" or "union". In other words, a point where maximum physical effort meets up with total determination (will-power or "spirit"). It concentrates every part of you into one split-second action. The shout also acts to contract the stomach muscles and give a stronger base for your techniques, and it can also distract or momentarily startle your opponent into leaving an opening for your strike. It can also channel your fear into working for you, rather than against you, strengthening your action rather than allowing you to fall apart into non-action. So, don't feel silly, KIAI!

Q Should children practise in the same way as grown-ups?

A No! You must understand that there are many differences, not only between children's bodies and adults' bodies, but also between boys' bodies and girls' bodies, and even between people of the same age and sex.

Q What do you mean, Master?

A Well, for example, by the time that they reach the age of six, most girls are physically more mature than boys, and, indeed, by the age of thirteen or fourteen they are some two years in advance. You might have noticed that many girls up to their early teens are as strong as boys of the same age. After puberty (the period when children's bodies mature into young adults' bodies) this tends to change, and boys will develop more muscular strength than girls, but may tend to lose their flexibility more; boys of this age will also show a greater degree of co-ordination than girls.

Q Master, why do I seem to be able to get a technique right for a little while, and then, all of a sudden it seems to go all wrong?

A Well. You must remember what I said above, and realise that your own physical development is unique to you. You may develop regularly, and continually adapt your technique to your growth, or – more likely – you will grow in fits and starts, and this will make you feel clumsy for a time. But don't worry, it is natural and you will soon adapt.

Questions to the Master

Q Master, what is the most important thing to remember?

A It is both simple and most difficult. "Be true to yourself!" Do not let yourself down, in training and in your life. Train honestly and do not expect any reward except to know that you have done your best.

Q Will I have to harden my hands and break boards or bricks?

A Certainly not! It would be foolish and unnecessary to go to such lengths. You will practise striking a bag or pad, to learn how to give blows without injuring yourself, but for a young person to strike anything hard is sheer folly!

20 Questions to the Master

Q Will I have to take part in competitions?

A Well, eventually, yes! Not necessarily fighting in championships, but at some stage you will have to learn what it is like to be put under pressure, so that in a difficult situation you will be better prepared to act correctly without being influenced by fear or nervousness.

This may be just at your regular gradings to begin with, but eventually you will be expected to test your skill against (or with the help of) another young student. You will probably find that you will really enjoy competition, once you get used to it; and of course it will be carefully controlled by your *Sensei*, and any dangerous techniques –

A

B

E

F

Questions to the Master 21

Examples of pad work:

A Oi-zuki   **E** Mae-geri

B Oi-zuki   **F** Mae-geri

C Gyaku-zuki   **G** Mawashi-geri

D Gyaku-zuki   **H** Mawashi-geri

C

D

G

H

Questions to the Master

aiming to strike the head or vital areas, for example – are forbidden.

There are also **Kata** competitions, where you and others do your *Kata* in front of judges, and are given marks according to how well you have performed.

From learning how it feels to be in these situations you will gain self-confidence, and be better able to deal with all the many problems and difficulties you will experience in daily life, and there is no doubt that young people who train correctly in Karate do become more alert, confident and self-reliant, and able to keep a clear head when dealing with matters outside the *Dojo*.

Q Master, do I have to watch my diet, or become a vegetarian or something?

A No! Just make sure that you don't only eat hamburgers and chips all the time.

Remember that not only is your body developing but you are also stressing it with training. This is very good for it, but just as an engine only works with the correct fuel, so it is that you owe it to your body to provide it with fresh fruit, greens and roughage and to make sure that your "fuel" is the correct type.

Of course, you should *never* smoke cigarettes or take any form of drugs which have not been prescribed for you by your doctor! In some ways young people are led into smoking cigarettes and experimenting with glue-sniffing and other forms of drug abuse, because their foolish friends try to convince them that it is somehow clever to do this. **IT ISN'T!**

Even in the sporting world some top-class, even Olympic champion, athletes have been led into taking drugs to try and make them become bigger and stronger, and perform better. In the end, however, even if, on the face of it, they seem successful in winning trophies they actually do a lot of harm to their bodies, often harm that cannot be undone! And they are *Cheats*!

The Martial Ways are based upon the idea of inner strength and self-reliance; this can never be achieved when you are having to rely on outside elements like alcohol or drugs to help you to cope!

Q How many times a week should I practise?

A As often as you are able without becoming obsessive and disturbing your daily life. Probably two to three times a week is best, but of course you might be taking part in other sports activities which will also help you to become fitter and stronger.

Q How long will a lesson last?

A In general there is little need for a young person's class to last for more than about one hour. It should begin with some warming-up exercises, some basic stretches, move on to some games-type activity and some Karate technique practice, and end with some cooling-down exercises and a short meditation period.

Q Master what is "The Karate Promise"?

Questions to the Master

A Ah yes. The **Kun**. This is traditionally recited in the *Dojo* before training, and serves to remind us that the Martial Arts are there to be used wisely and to guard us against their misuse.

There are various different versions of the following *Dojo Kun*, which is fairly typical and is often to be found in licences. It is sometimes recited in class, and serves to focus the attention on the serious nature of the study of the Martial Ways:

"I promise to uphold the true spirit of Karate-do, and never to use the skills that I am taught against any persons except for the defence of myself, family and friends in the instance of extreme danger or unprovoked attack, or in the support of Law and Order."

Q Is there anything to look for to show whether the club I want to join is a good or bad one?

A That is a good question! First, ask your parents to try and find out about the instructor: what are his qualifications? What do other members of his classes think? Do they enjoy the classes? Does he or she seem to be "into" his classes or does he merely stand in front issuing directions?

Again, look at the practice area itself. Is it clean and uncluttered? Are there proper changing facilities etc? Are there mats available for use?

Your parents should also make sure that first-aid facilities are on hand, and that the club runs a proper licensing and insurance scheme. These things should help you to decide.

Q Can you explain a little more about the grading system, Master?

A Of course. I have already said that generally every three months students undergo a test to see if they are ready to receive a higher **Kyu** grade and wear a different colour belt to signify their standard. This isn't a competition, where one wins and the other loses. All who are good enough will pass.

Questions to the Master

Most gradings begin with an examination of basic stances and techniques, moving from the most basic to the more advanced, depending on the grade attempted. Then there is usually a test of attacking and defensive pre-arranged practice with a partner. Finally the student has to perform one (or, in some instances, two) *Kata*.

Each section is marked by a senior examiner, and a record made of a student's strong and weak points. Provided he or she has progressed satisfactorily a further *Kyu* grade is awarded.

Q How many of these *Kyu* grades are there, Master, and what colour are the belts?

A Well, that depends upon the particular Association or School; but to take The Federation of Shotokan Karate as an example, there are 9 *Kyu* grades, beginning at 9th and progressing to 1st. Then come the Black-belt ***Dan*** grades, starting with 1st and advancing (at least in theory) to 10th. For a long time, though, you will have to concentrate on progressing through the *Kyu* grades. The *Kyu* colours are as follows:

9th Red
8th Orange
7th Yellow
6th Green
5th Purple
4th Purple with white stripe
3rd Brown
2nd Brown with white stripe
1st Brown with two white stripes.

Then come the Black-belt grades. (Do not, by the way, be misled by thinking that all Black-belts are – by definition – experts. "*Dan*" means, literally, "step"; thus a 1st *Dan* has taken the first step towards being a serious student. It is most unlikely that any real mastery could be claimed by anyone with fewer than 20 years' practice at least!)

Q Master, in self-defence what is the most important thing to remember?

A There are two things. *Get away!* and make as *much noise as possible* by *yelling, shouting and screaming!*

You should never try to win a fight with an attacker, just fight to get free and then shout and run. You should practise this in class – even the shouting!

Questions to the Master

Q Master, whenever I have to do a *Kata* in front of my teacher, or enter a competition, I feel scared and often have to keep going to the lavatory, and I get very tense! What should I do?

A Be very grateful! All those signs show that your body is working exactly as it should!

There is an automatic response in the human body to moments of tension which doctors call: the "fight or flight response". This means that the body is gearing itself up to deal with an emergency situation which might require you to run away or fight your way out of danger. In the days of the cavemen this helped them to escape from becoming a dinosaur's dinner!

Nowadays there are no more dinosaurs, but whenever we are a bit frightened our bodies act in the same way. All sorts of things happen, from your heart beating faster to your mouth getting dry, and you feel that you want to go to the lavatory. This shows that you have now become better prepared to take action. Remember that fear is only an emotion, it has a job to do, it "switches on" the body's systems. It moves you from your normal state to over-drive.

So, now that you understand what is happening you will not need to worry when you feel like that again!

26 Questions to the Master

Q Master, I know that you have talked about the nervousness that we feel before a contest, and that we should realise that this is natural, but I actually get *scared*!

A Well. I'm sure that you have heard of Mike Tyson, one of the world's most feared and formidable heavyweight champion boxers? Now his trainer was a famous man called Cus D'Amato, and he used to tell Mike that the difference between a hero and a coward was not in how they felt, but in how they acted. Both were afraid; the coward, however, refused to face up to what had to be faced, whereas the more disciplined hero – although just as afraid – fought off his fear and faced up to the task ahead. There was no difference in the way they felt, only in how they acted!

Q Master, do you have any particular favourite saying that could help us?

A Well, I don't claim that it's original, but I've always had a fondness for: "It is better to light a candle than to complain of the dark." This means that instead of just complaining about something you should try and do something about it!

Thank you Master!

Types of Activities

Remember that training for young students has to be different from that of adults, because young people's bodies cannot physically cope with the same stresses nor can their minds concentrate on one thing for as long.

WARM-UP AND STRETCHING EXERCISES

You should always warm-up thoroughly with some simple aerobic type exercises before starting to stretch. Even if you don't feel cold you must warm-up properly, so that your muscles become more pliable and less prone to injury.

A lot of research has been done into discovering the safest and most effective way of increasing flexibility, and you should try never to "bounce" into any stretch positions; just pull yourself gently into them and hold them for a few seconds at a time.

Don't forget, as a young person you should already be fairly flexible, so don't try too hard to increase your range without doing exercises to strengthen the muscles as well. Overstretching without strengthening can cause problems in adult years!

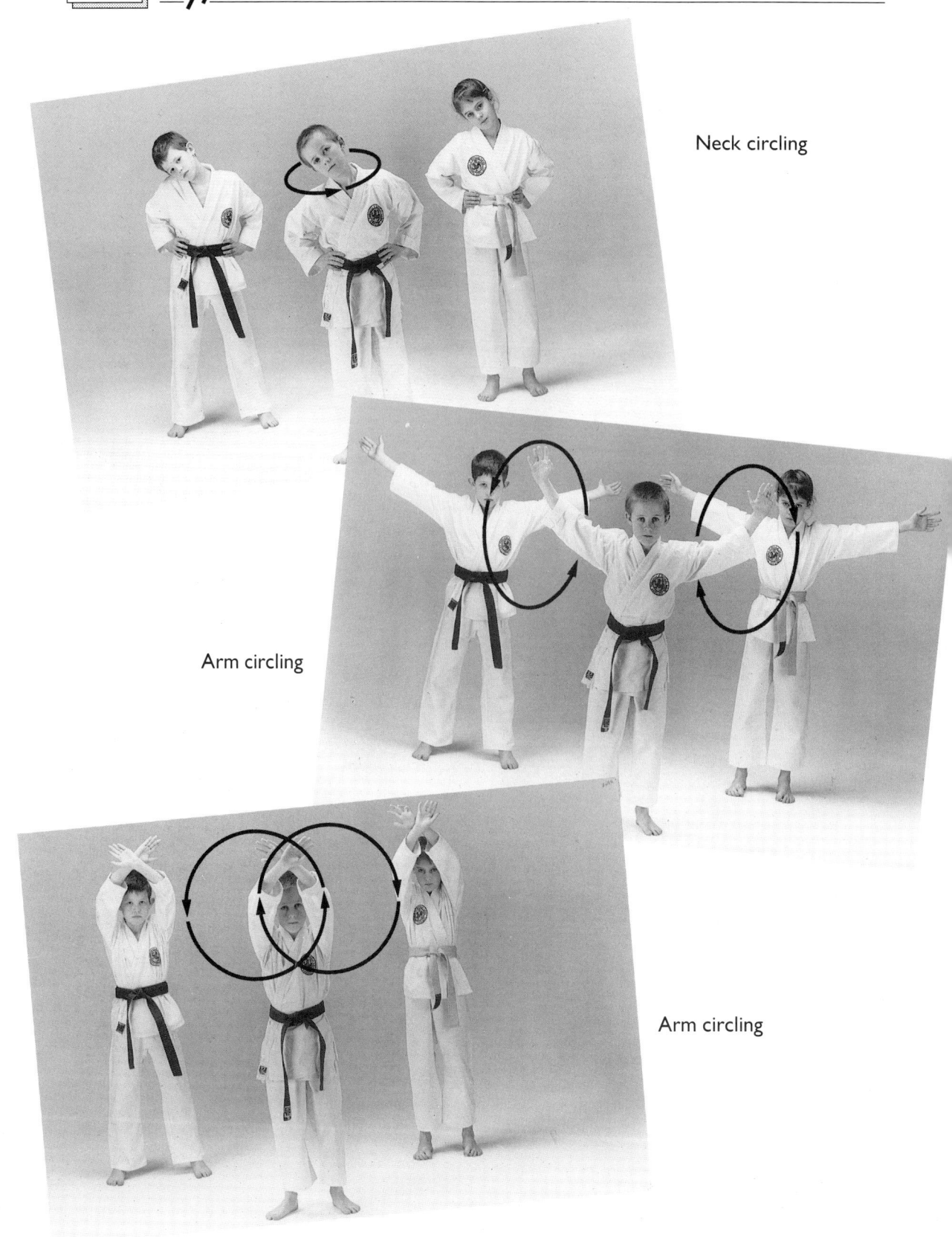

28 Types of Activities

Neck circling

Arm circling

Arm circling

Types of Activities 29

Waist circling

Knee circling

30　Types of Activities

Leg stretching exercises

Types of Activities 31

Leg stretching exercises

32 Types of Activities

Hip stretching exercises

Types of Activities 33

Front and side splits

34 Types of Activities

Hamstring and inner thigh stretches, plus waist twist

Types of Activities

36 Types of Activities

Front and side leg swinging

Right: Arm wrestling

Types of Activities

CROSS-TRAINING EXERCISES

Some of the skills needed in the Martial Arts can be developed by what is called "cross-training". That is, by other activities which can be used as a break from the regular training, but which will, none the less, give practice in co-ordination, body-shifting and spatial awareness, which are vital components of regular training. Strength, stamina and flexibility can also be enhanced by suitable team activities and partner work such as:

- Arm wrestling. Lie on the floor, grasp each other's opposite hand and without jerking try to force your partner's hand over.
- Wheelbarrow races. Carrying your partner by the legs, race from one side of the *Dojo* to the other, then change positions and race back again.

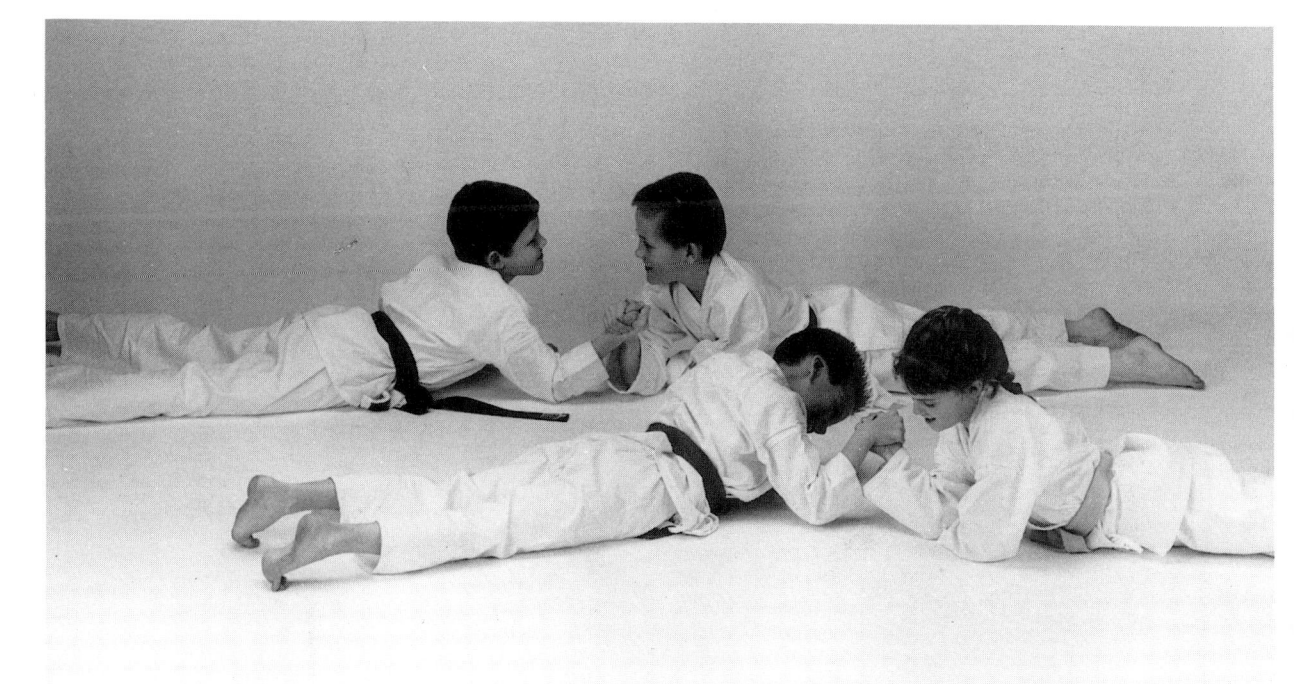

38 Types of Activities

Wheelbarrow races

Balance training on one leg

- Hopping fights. Hold one foot up with one hand and try to make your partner put both feet on the floor by pushing or pulling.

Types of Activities 39

- Squat fights. Squat with one arm behind your back and attempt to unbalance your partner using your other hand. You may not stand up. Best of three wins.

Balance and leg strengthening training

40 Types of Activities

A

B

C

D

E

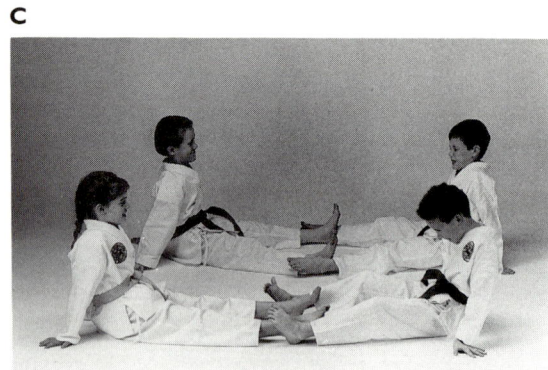

- Wrist-to-wrist tension exercise. Stand with your arms held out at shoulder height to the front. Your partner places his/her wrists on the outside of your wrists and slowly tries to touch them together. You must try to keep the wrists from coming together. Then change arm positions and repeat.

A & B Squeeze arms together

C Squeeze legs together

D & E Get to your feet!

Types of Activities

- Leg-to-leg tension exercise. Both sit on the floor, legs apart, facing each other. Place your ankles outside your partner's and try to force them together while your opponent strives to keep them apart. Switch leg positions and repeat.
- One partner lies down and the other gets on top and takes a firm hold, the supine partner must struggle to regain a standing position, whilst the other tries to keep him/her down.
- Team leapfrog races. From one side of the *Dojo* to the other and back. First team to finish wins.

All these and other related activities can properly form part of regular training.

SELF-DEFENCE

Sessions can be varied by the inclusion of basic self-defence practice for children, and "awareness" discussions. The *Sensei* will find that these discussions can usefully take place in the rest periods following high intensity exercise.

Of course, you should realise that self-defence doesn't just refer to techniques to escape from holds, and so on. No! Actually it begins with being aware of situations which in some cases could lead you into danger in the world outside the *Dojo*, such as accepting a lift in a car with someone you do not know, even if they tell you that your parents have asked them to collect you. You *must not* go with them, nor should you encourage strangers to talk to you, and *never* take presents or sweets from them.

Again, if you are bullied by anyone you should tell them firmly and *loudly* to stop, and that you are going to tell an adult; and if they continue to harass you then you *must* tell either your teacher or your parents. Don't be afraid to tell. Nothing can be done about a problem if it is kept hidden! There is more detailed advice on this matter in the section which begins on page 93.

Techniques

A Shizentai – yoi

B Kiba-dachi

C Kokutsu-dachi

D Zenkutsu-dachi

Disallowed techniques

There are some Karate techniques which are too dangerous for young people to practise, for a number of reasons; they may demand a degree of control which a young body is not yet capable of, and could therefore be dangerous to the receiving partner; or they might throw an unwelcome strain upon the ligaments, tendons, joints and muscles of the growing body which could have unfortunate effects in years to come.

There are some techniques which are also dangerous even for adults to practise, and great care must be taken not to hurt your partner.

You should *not*: attack the groin, kick to the knee joints, or strike the face, eyes or neck. Nor should you attempt any strangle or choke holds, or locks against the joints. Do *not* attempt any sweep or throw except as directed by your *Sensei*, and then only upon matted surfaces.

Breakfall techniques

All Judo students have to learn to breakfall, and it is a very good idea for young *Karate-ka* to practise them also, as there are throwing and sweeping techniques in Karate, and it is important to be used to "rough and tumble" so as not to be disorientated or injured if thrown.

Stances

The stances in Karate are very important, so it is worth your while spending a lot of time mastering them. Once done this will make everything else that much easier!

The basic idea is to make sure that you have a strong base from which to perform your blocks and counters. You cannot strike hard, for example, if you are falling over your feet at the time!

Try to imagine a triangle or pyramid, with the widest part at the bottom. This will be very hard to push over or unbalance. Turn it up the other way, however, with the base in the air and the tip at the bottom, and this is obviously far more unstable. Try to be like the pyramid in the first case, with a firm, strong base.

The main point to remember whenever you are moving, is to try and keep your hips at the same height as you step. Do not bob up and down. This will enable you to move smoothly and quickly.

Techniques 43

A

B

C

D

Techniques

BLOCKS

You will mostly begin by using the little-finger edge of your open hand or the inside and outside of your forearms to block with. (Don't practise hard blocks for too long with a partner at first or you will find that your arms will become bruised and sore; eventually you will become used to this, and it will not hurt so much.)

There are three terms to learn which describe the area of the body to protect or attack. They are: *Jodan* (upper level), *Chudan* (middle level) and *Gedan* (lower level).

To begin with you will practise one main *Jodan* block called **Age-uke**, two *Chudan* blocks, from inside to outside called **Uchi-uke**, and from outside to inside called **Soto-ude-uke**. The main lower level block is called **Gedan-barai** (downward sweep).

Gedan barai and age-uke: Yoi

Raise hand

Step forward

Techniques 45

Gedan barai

Gedan barai

Step forward

Block – age-uke

Techniques

Soto-ude-uke: Gedan barai

Uchi-ude-uke: Gedan barai

Step forward

Techniques 47

Step forward

Zenkutsu-dachi
soto-ude-uke

Zenkutsu-dachi
uchi-ude-uke

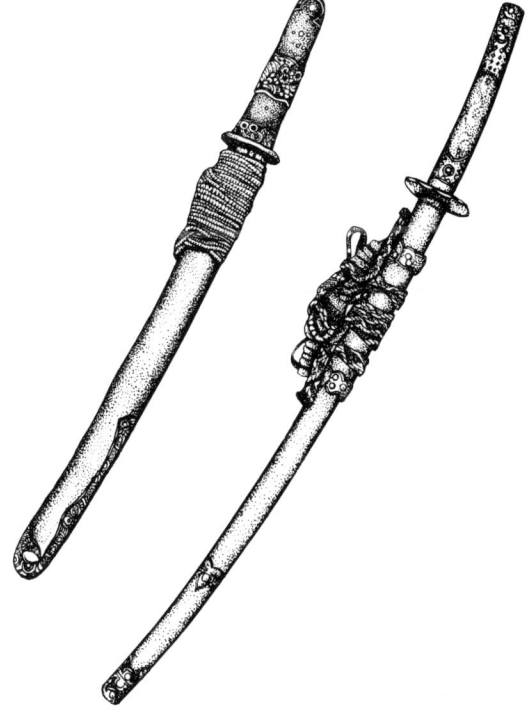

48 Techniques

Shuto-uke: Yoi

Prepare hands

Right: Step forward kokutsu-dachi shuto-uke

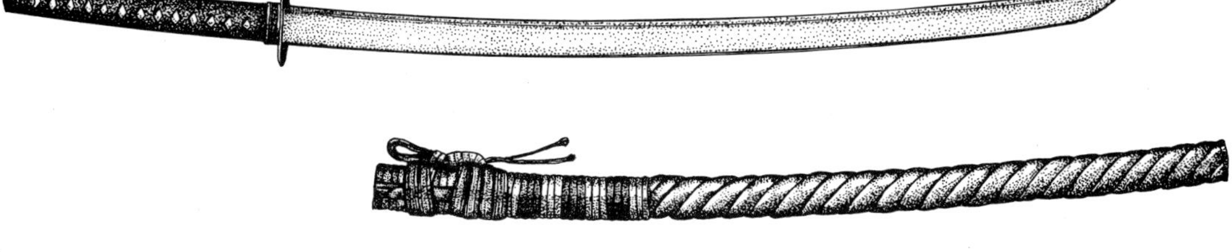

Techniques 49

50 Techniques

Punches

The first thing you must learn is how to make a fist properly so that you will not hurt yourself when you punch. With your hand open, fingers together like a spear, and beginning with your little finger, fold your fingers into the palm of your hand, then fold the thumb over them. Do not let it stick out or it will get knocked and that can be very painful!

Most (but not all!) Karate punches travel in a straight line to their target and contact with the area around the two large knuckles. The basic punch (*Zuki*) is delivered from the hip with the back of the fist downwards, twisting in a corkscrew motion so that the back of the fist is upwards just before impact. As one fist shoots out, so the other is pulled back strongly. This adds power to the technique.

Remember to make sure that your wrist is not bent, otherwise you may damage it when making contact with a bag (even a soft bag or an airshield). This is important if you want powerful punches. Most people cannot punch with all their power at a bag because they would injure themselves.

Making a fist:

A Extend fingers

B Curl in first joints

C Completely curl fingers

D Press down thumb

E Correct position

F Incorrect

G Incorrect

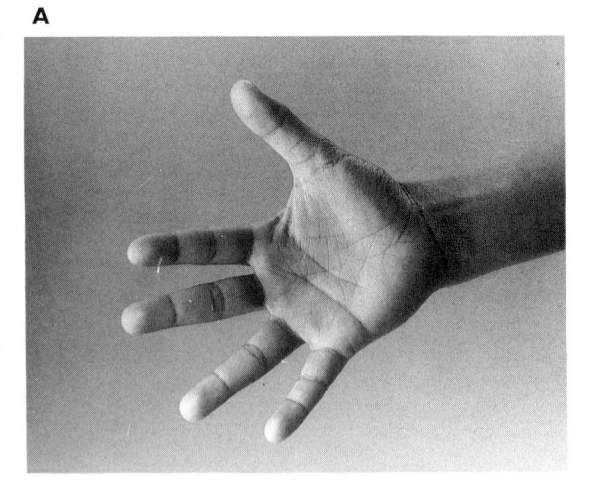

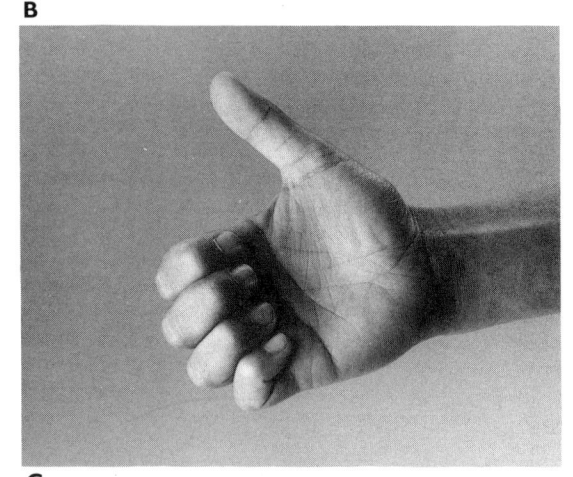

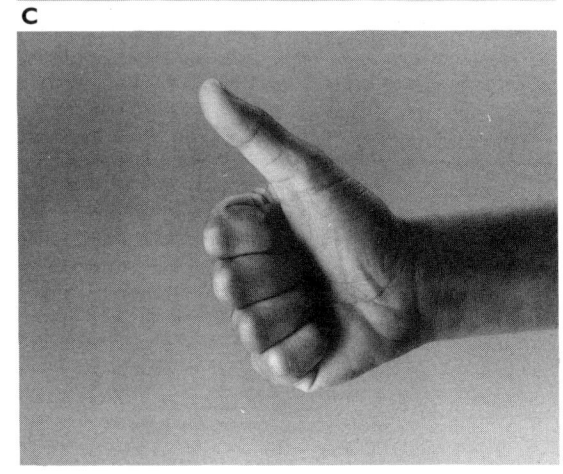

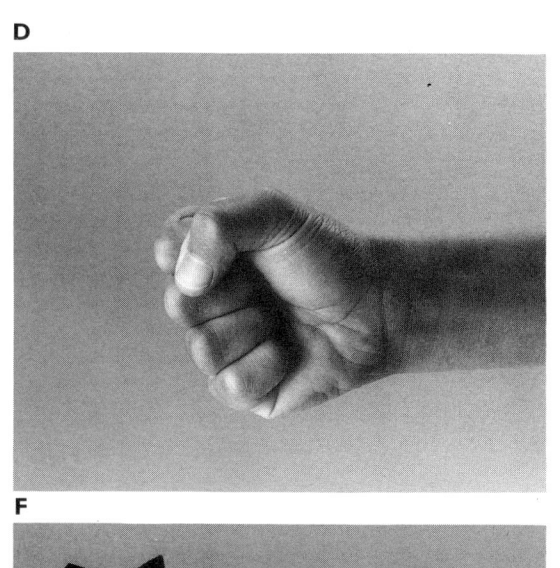

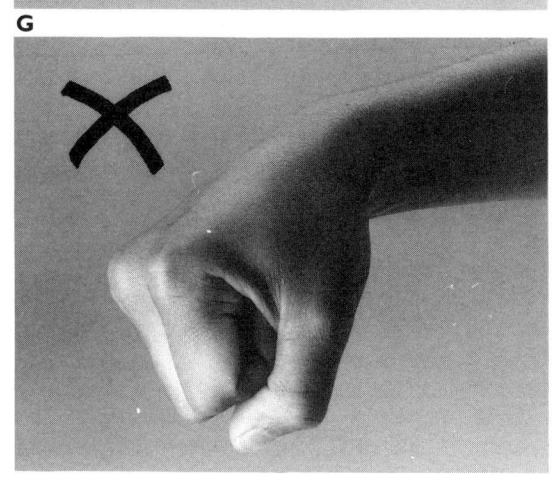

Techniques 51

D

E

F ✗

G ✗

52 Techniques

A

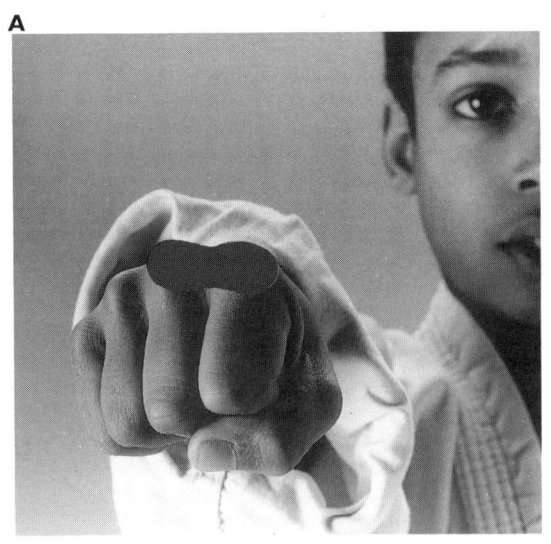

B

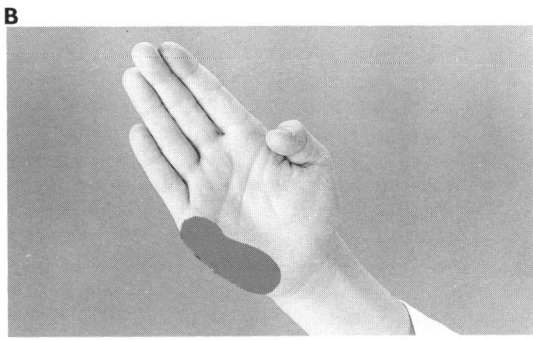

C

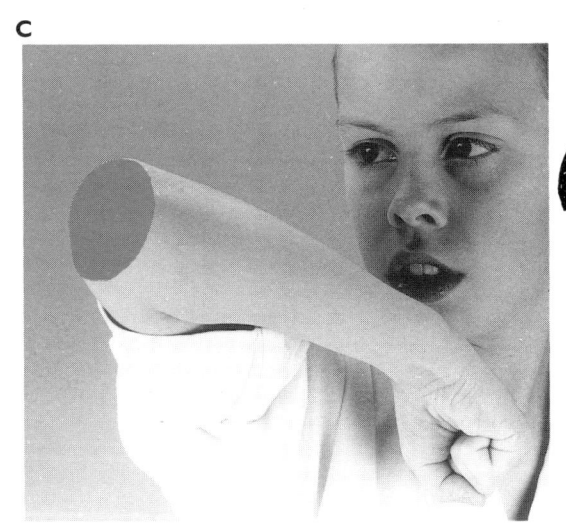

As you punch you should breathe out, and just at the moment of contact you should sharply tighten your stomach and your muscles for just an instant before relaxing and breathing in as you rapidly pull back your punching arm. This is called "focus" (*Kime* in Japanese), and is very important.

Note that although in Karate most of the punches travel in a straight line, this is because the punchers are trained. In a self-defence situation it is important to remember that the most popular punch used by an untrained person is a hook or a wild swing. You should be sure to practise blocking this type of attack, because you need to modify your technique so as not to be hit.

Also, make sure that you often practise elbow-strike counters, as even a small young person can, with training, deliver a powerful blow with the elbow, which has the advantage of being difficult to damage.

The striking surfaces:
A First two knuckles
B Edge of open hand
C The striking surface of the elbow
D & E Choku-zuki

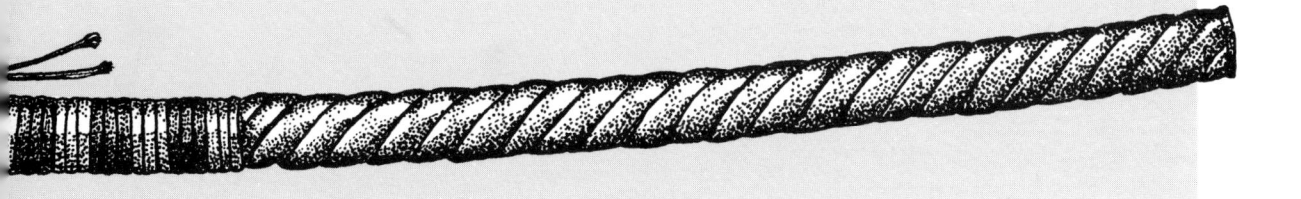

Techniques 53

D   E

54 Techniques

A

B

C

D

Techniques 55

A Oi-zuki and gyaku-zuki Zentkutsu-dachi
E Step up
C Step forward
D Punch
E Punch gyaku-zuki

E

KICKS

The kicking techniques are characteristic of the Eastern Martial Arts, and – unlike in the West, where it was often considered ungentlemanly to use the feet – are used with considerable effect and power.

There are four parts of the foot used to strike the target:
- The ball of the foot, exposed by pulling back the toes. (This is the part in contact with the ground when you stand on tip-toe.)

Striking surfaces:
Ball of foot

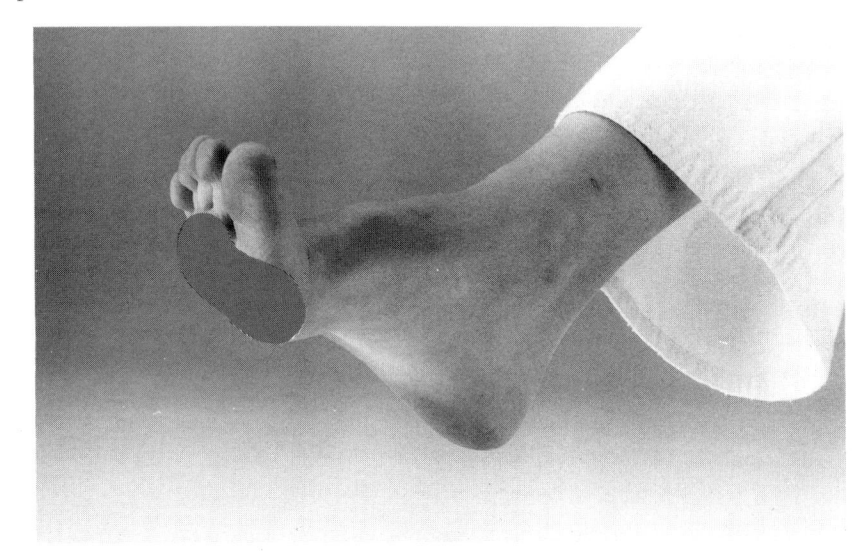

Side of foot

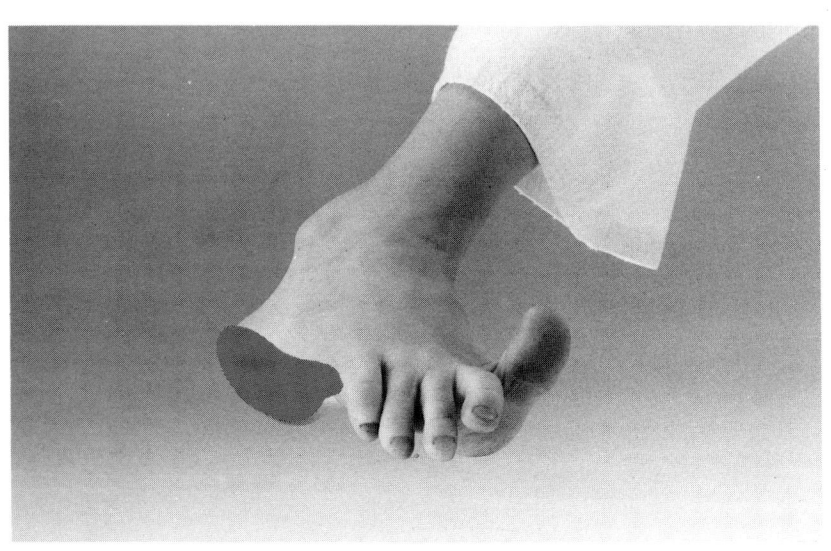

- The top of the foot, made strong by pointing the toes and squeezing them together. (But be careful, it can really hurt if you hit a hard pointed object like an elbow!)
- The outside edge, which is used to attack the limbs.
- The heel or bottom of the foot, generally used to attack the head, mid-section or legs.

Instep

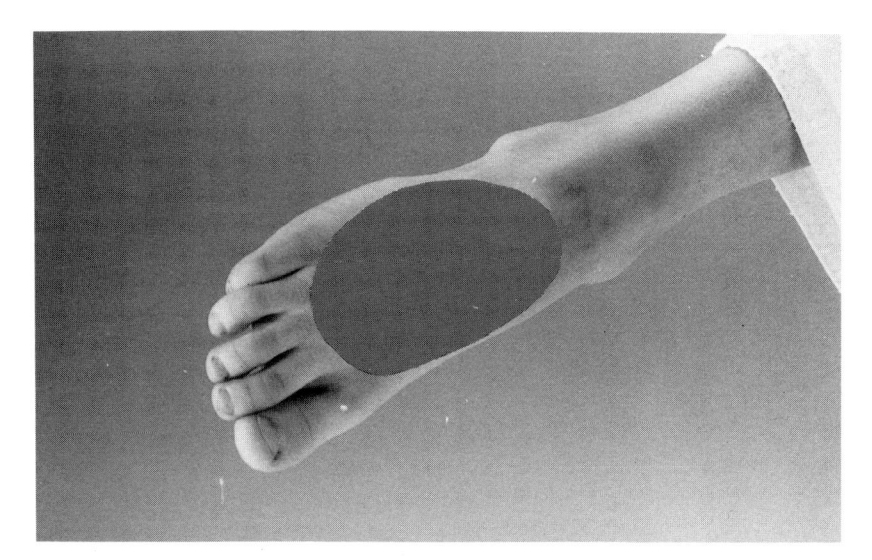

Heel

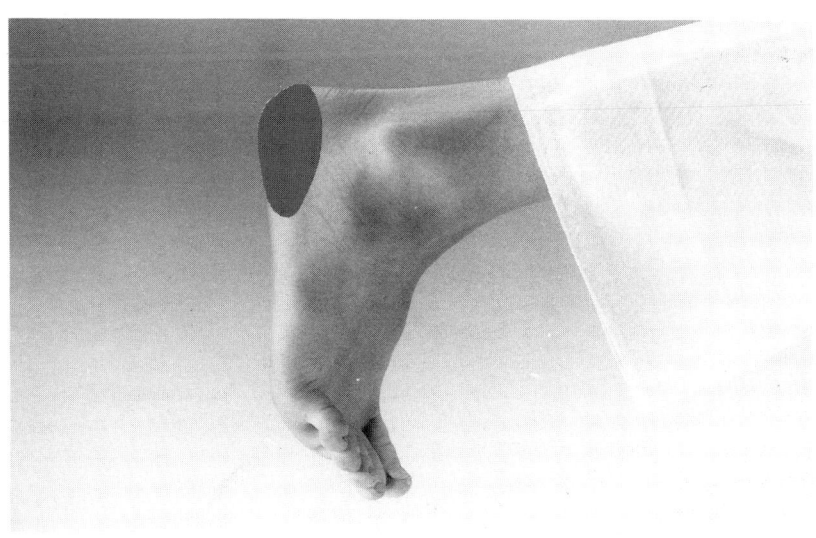

Techniques

The main point to remember when practising your kicks is to raise your knee high no matter what kick you are going to use, and to pull the kicking leg back quickly to keep your balance. You should also try to maintain your guard at all times during the kick, because should it fail, or be blocked, your opponent could take advantage of your poor guard to press home his or her counter technique.

A very good form of practice is to do three consecutive kicks, one to the front, one to the side and one to the rear, without putting your kicking leg down. This will really test your balance and muscular control! Remember to practise with each leg, not just your better one.

Mae-geri: Zenkutsu-dachi

Lift knee

Right: Mae-geri

Techniques 59

60 Techniques

A

B

Yoko-geri-keagi:
A Kiba-dachi
B Step over

Techniques 61

C

D

C Raise knee

D Yoko-geri-keage

Techniques

Yoko-geri-kekomi:
Kiba-dachi

Step over

Techniques 63

Raise knee

Yoko-geri-kekomi

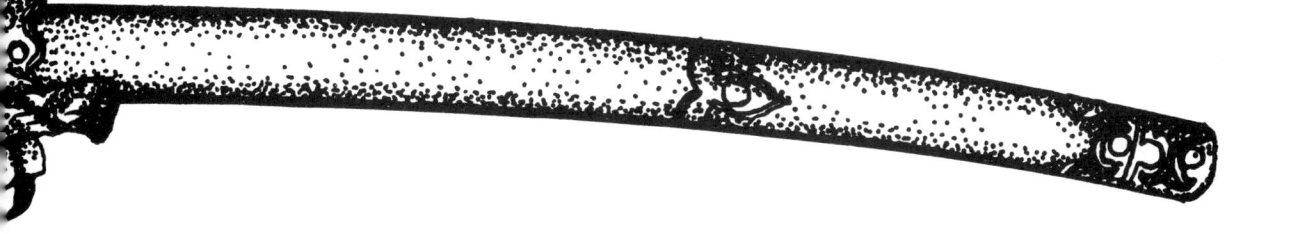

64 Techniques

Mawashi-geri:
Zenkutsu-dachi

… Techniques 65

Raise knee

Mawashi-geri

Techniques

Ushiro-geri:
- **A** Zenkutsu-dachi
- **B** Turn
- **C** Turn head
- **D** Ushiro-geri

Techniques 67

D

SOLO PRACTICE

When you begin to practise the techniques of Karate, be they blocks, kicks, punches or strikes, you will be doing them into the empty air, and it is important that you do not allow your arm or leg to over-extend. That is to snap it out with such force that you place too much stress on the elbow or knee joint.

You should try to make sure that neither your arm nor leg is thrust completely straight, by tightening your muscles at almost full extension to ensure that it keeps very slightly bent. This will prevent damage to the joint and also help with your "focus".

PARTNER WORK AND SPARRING

You cannot learn Karate properly without practising with a partner. Because Karate techniques are potentially dangerous, however, this practice is traditionally structured into specific types of partner work, which are more or less the same no matter what type of Karate you are learning.

Basically you will begin by facing your partner, who should be roughly the same age and size as you, and normally of about the same degree of skill. Then, to the count of your teacher, one will practise a punch or kick whilst the other will practise an appropriate block. This is called **Kihon-ippon-kumite** or basic one-step sparring.

Techniques 69

Kihon-ippon-kumite:
Musubi-dachi

Rei

Yoi shizentai

Gedan barai

Oi-zuki
block age-uke

Pull back front foot

Mae-geri

Age-empi

72 Techniques

Gedan barai

Chudan oi-zuki
Heisoku-dachi block

Techniques 73

Yoko-geri-kekomi

Gyaku-zuki

Techniques

Gedan barai

Mae-geri
gedan barai block

Far right:
Mawashi-geri

Techniques 75

Techniques

When you are competent at this you will practise five attacks consecutively to the head whilst your partner moves back defending. After the fifth attack your partner will counter-punch. Then the roles will be reversed, with your partner attacking and you defending. This will be repeated with the mid-section as the target. This is called: **Gohon-kumite**, or "five-step" in English.

There are also other pre-arranged forms of practice called "three-step" sparring and "one-step" sparring; and – as you become more experienced – "semi-free" sparring in which the techniques are specified in advance, but both *Karate-ka* are free to move around and attack whenever an opening is perceived.

Finally, for the more advanced student there is **Ju-kumite**, "free-style" sparring, where nothing is pre-arranged, but care must be taken not to hurt your partner. You should not be practising "free-style" until you are very experienced, as it can actually lead to many bad habits which will hold you back in the long run!

A

Jodan:

A Start position
B Rei
C Yoi and gedan barai
D Right oi-zuki/age-uke

Left oi-zuki/age-uke **E**

Right oi-zuki/age-uke **F**

Left oi-zuki/age uke **G**

Right oi-zuki/age-uke

Counter punch gyaku-zuki.
Kiai!

KIAI

80 Techniques

Chudan:
Start position

Right oi-zuki, soto-ude-uke

A

B

Techniques 81

Left oi-zuki, soto-ude-uke

C

Right oi-zuki, soto-ude-uke

D

82 Techniques

E

F

Techniques

G

E Left oi-zuki, soto-ude-uke
F Right oi-zuki, soto-ude-uke
G Counter punch gyaku-zuki. *Kiai!*

KATA

There is no simple translation for the word *Kata*. At first glance someone performing a *Kata* looks almost as though they are engaged in some sort of ritual and powerful dance routine! In fact *Kata* exist in many of the Japanese and Okinawan Martial Arts. Often created by masters many years ago they are actually series of movements and techniques giving practice in defending against a number of imaginary assailants, and in the use of dangerous counter-attacks which could not be used against an actual partner without causing serious damage.

All *Karate-ka* have to learn the *Kata*, and there are – for example – some 26 different ones in Shotokan, each of a varying degree of difficulty and concentrating on different aspects for the student to practise. The *Kata* act in the manner of alphabets, only of techniques instead of letters, and help the student to practise properly even if the *Sensei* is not present.

To begin with you will learn them in a group, slowly and by count. Then, when you can remember the sequences, you will perform them either in a group or on your own until you master them. You will normally have to perform a *Kata* (or two) as part of your regular gradings.

There are also *Kata* competitions that you can enter, when your performance will be judged and points awarded. When doing a *Kata* try at all times to imagine that you can see your opponents and the attacks that they are making on you. This will make your practice more realistic. Also try to make sure that your movements are smooth and not rushed.

Always begin and end your *Kata* with a bow. (*Rei*).

(Although initially the *Kata* appear to be fairly simple and obvious this is not always the case, especially with the more advanced, which often contain "hidden" techniques, where the obvious obscures the more sophisticated. A good understanding of the **Bunkai** (applications) is necessary in order to gain most from your *Kata* practice.)

Techniques

Deep concentration shows on this young competitor's face as he performs his kata at the British Championships at Crystal Palace

Despite the large audience this young competitor completes his kata – Las Vegas, USA

Competition

Although to begin with there were no contests in Karate, because it was considered to be purely a potentially deadly fighting art, students soon began to want to test their skills against one another. But in so doing they realised that for safety's sake they had to make some changes, and make some target areas (and some techniques) illegal.

So, rules were devised, and soon properly organised local, national and international championships were regularly held. Indeed, Karate has now been introduced into the Olympic arena.

The majority of international events tend to fall into two main categories, those of the WUKO (World Union of Karate) and the JKA (Japan Karate Association). The main difference being that WUKO events are won by scoring a maximum of 3 full-points or 6 near-points, whilst the JKA require only 1 full-point or 2 near-points to win.

The reason for the difference is that the chance to win with one full-point keeps the contest close to its original idea of one deadly blow defeating an attacker. This can lead to unadventurous contests, when one error can lose the match. To make contests more exciting some groups changed the rules so that more interesting techniques could be attempted.

The strength of Karate in Great Britain can be judged from the fact that British teams are

Vince Morris takes juniors through five-step sparring during a grading examination in Torquay

consistently the winners in international matches of both WUKO and JKA events!

Most Karate groups and associations hold regular championships, ranging from local to national, even to international, to allow the students to compete in *Kata* and *Kumite* events, and these normally include junior categories.

If you are asked to take part in a competition, remember that you don't *have* to. No-one should be forced or pressurised into taking part, although most students really enjoy them.

Competitions should simply be a part of your training, giving opportunities to test your skill and temperament, and they should always be tightly controlled, and under the supervision of a senior and experienced chief referee.

Again, it is definitely not a good idea for relative beginners to take part in the fighting events. They do not have the skill, nor the control, and can be a danger to themselves and to their opponents.

All the contestants should be familiar with the rules of the competition, and all the junior entrants should make sure that every effort has been taken to ensure their safety. There should be height, weight, age and grade restrictions in force to make sure that no-one is over-matched and therefore at a significant disadvantage. All *Kumite* competitors should have to wear proper mits, and *no* contact to the head should be allowed at all. Needless to say, all *Kumite* should take place upon a proper matted area.

You should not take part in any *Kumite* match which entails boys fighting against girls. *Kata* events are different.

Of course, medical and first-aid attention should be available upon demand.

Try to remember that Karate is an art, not just a sport, and whether you are taking part or supporting a friend who is competing, you should maintain a good standard of behaviour, with no arguing with referees or calling out unseemly remarks. Never be disrespectful. A healthy rivalry is one thing, shouting derogatory or abusive comments is quite another entirely.

As a competitor you will soon learn that no referee – no matter how good and experienced – can *always* make the right decision. Karate techniques are often so fast that occasionally a blow or a block will be missed, and sometimes a score awarded or disallowed which you might feel is unfair. This cannot be helped, because the whole idea of judging the winner of a fight by awarding points rather than by seeing who it is that survives is artificial, and therefore open to error.

You should realise that:
(a) next time the "wrong" decision is just as likely to be in your favour as not
(b) being judged the winner is not the primary objective in Martial Arts competitions, the idea being for you to test yourself under stress
(c) providing you have done your very best, you can never have come away as a loser.

Of course to lose a championship on a bad decision is always upsetting, and all good referees will do their utmost to make sure that mistakes are few and far between. Nevertheless, life being what it is, nobody is perfect, so sometimes you will have to swallow your disappointment, and learn to deal with those "two imposters: Success and Failure!"

THE COMPETITION RULES AND AREA

Practically all associations have competitions, and the rules vary from style to style. All, however, should make sure that proper medical facilities are available, and that the safety of the competitors comes first.

You should ask your *Sensei* to explain the rules carefully to you, and ask questions if you don't understand.

You should be in weight, age and/or size categories, so a really big person is not fighting a really small one. You should be wearing padded mits, possibly shinpads, and a groin protector, but you should check this out with your teacher. There should be no head contact, and only controlled body contact.

There must be proper medical attention available, not simply junior first-aiders or the like.

Competition 89

A junior competition in Las Vegas, USA. Note the fist mitts

TAKING PART IN A COMPETITION

Competitions are nerve-racking! Especially your first few. You will undoubtedly feel nervous, but so will *everybody* else. We are including this report by one of our young members, just so that you can see that you will not be alone in how you feel.

Competition

My First Competition   by Neil Sutcliffe   aged 12 (3rd Kyu)

I was terribly nervous when we arrived in Rotherham. I had entered in the under-12-year-olds Team Kata event, and the Individual and Team Kumite.

My two partners and I had chosen to perform Hean Godan for our Kata, and had only been practising for about two weeks prior to the competition. My heart was beating rapidly as we marched on to the mat. "Here goes", I thought. I looked the referee straight in the eyes as I shouted "Hean Godan!" One - Two - I started. My arms and legs moved like clockwork and I could see out of the corner of my eye that my partners were with me. Good! As we came to rest in our final positions I felt confident that we hadn't made any mistakes.

The marks were given – not bad – and a cheer went up from our club supporters as we made our way off the mat. The other teams completed their kata and were then asked to stand to find out who was going through to the finals.

The referee shouted: "Redhill Tigers!" That was us! I couldn't believe it, we were into the finals!

After a short break it was time for the individual Kumite. I felt sick as I walked over to the mat where I would be fighting. The time was ticking by as I waited and waited for my name to be called. Who was going to be my opponent? Would I remember the correct moves that I had been taught? If I didn't I would get hit!

My Dad was giving me words of encouragement as my name was called and I made my way onto

Competition

the mat. My opponent didn't look particularly mean, but I couldn't relax.

He made a dive for me and missed. I decided to wait and let him come in to me, telegraphing the move he was going to use. I side-stepped and went in and scored with a reverse punch. I thought about being adventurous and using a front kick, but decided against it as I might leave myself open for a hit?

Again he came in, and again I scored. This wasn't so bad after all!

I scored yet again, and suddenly it was over I had won my first round and my first ever fight!

As I waited for my next opponent fear started to creep back into me and I felt jittery as I listened to instructions and encouragement. Then I was back on the mat.

This opponent started off very lively, throwing punches and kicks everywhere, but missing. His Sensei told him to slow down, and so he just stood there waiting for me to make a move. I started moving from side to side feigning punches. I thought about going in a few times but uncertainty stopped me, and I waited a bit longer. I heard the 30 seconds bell. We both stood there looking at each other.

One of us had to make a move. Suddenly I leapt in with a reverse punch which fortunately landed right on target, giving me a ½ point, and winning me the match.

I walked off the mat and immediately burst into tears. Fear, excitement, disbelief were all rushing around in my head. My heart was pounding and I felt sick. I didn't want to go on. But I had to go on, I was through to the quarter-finals and I didn't want to let anybody down!

92 Competition

Neil's nerves finally got the better of him in his next fight, when he fought an opponent from a different style, whose coach helped to intimidate Neil by shouting remarks like: "Get him! Get him, he's easy!"

He tried to move, but his legs "turned to jelly", as Neil put it, and he could not regain his control.

> It was all over. I had lost the round. I walked off the mat choked, disappointed and drained. My parents were patting me on the back and telling me that I had done well, but I was frustrated and angry with myself for not trying harder.

At the end of the tournament Neil went home with a *Kata* trophy and a lot of experience to build on for the future.

When it is your turn, remember that you may be disappointed if you don't win your match, but as long as you have done your best, and you learn from the experience, you should never feel that you have lost!

One thing stands out from this insight into how it feels to take part in a competition for the first time, and that is how important it is to make your mind strong, and to be positive. Do not be over-awed by your opponent's appearance. Big body doesn't automatically mean big heart, or big skill, or anything at all. Be strong!!

The Tiger Club & Newsletter

Many associations have a special section or club for its younger members, and run competitions and newsletters often with a pen-pal column, so that the young *Karate-ka* throughout the association can learn about each other and get to know others with similar interests.

In the FSK the junior section has its own Tiger Club, with its distinctive logo, stickers, newsletter and membership card.

FINAL NOTE
Remember: learning karate is fun! Enjoy it!

Notes to Junior Karate-Ka

You have a right to protect yourself!

The Martial Arts evolved because people wanted to be able to protect themselves from harm. Unfortunately, the need for self-protection still exists in the world of today.

Practising the Martial Arts helps you to become more confident and self-reliant, and provides you with a skill which is there to help you if the need ever arises. A good Martial Artist, however, tries to ensure that bad situations are avoided before they become too dangerous. So you should try to follow the advice given below, and, without being silly about it, always try to take sensible precautions. Remember that you too have rights!

1 YOUR BODY BELONGS TO YOU!

There are a lot of strange people in the world, and part of growing up (unfortunately) is becoming aware of this.

Some grown-ups are unable to form satisfactory relationships with people of their own age, and sometimes use their adulthood to force themselves upon children. This is *illegal*.

You must remember that your body belongs to you! Just because someone is older than you this does not give them the right to touch you.

2 SAY NO!

Most children are taught to do what they are told by an adult, and this is normally OK. But sometimes it is right for you to say *NO* to anyone who tries to get you to do something that you feel is wrong, and that your parents would not like.

3 DON'T BE AFRAID TO TELL!

Sometimes young people are afraid to tell their parents or a teacher if something upsetting or bad has happened. Perhaps they feel that they will not be believed, or that they do not want to upset their parents. In all cases you *must tell*! Even if at first you are not believed, you must continue to tell a responsible person. This way you may even be saving another child from more serious harm.

Advice for Teenagers

1 SAY WHERE YOU ARE GOING

Do tell your parents where you are going and who you are going with, and if possible leave a contact number.

2 ONLY TRAVEL WITH SOMEONE YOU KNOW

If you do go out alone, to your Karate club, or a concert, or a dance etc., arrange definite transport with someone you know or with the organisers.

Also, if by some chance your transport home should not arrive, *do not* accept a lift with a stranger, no matter how nice they might seem. Use the telephone to make other arrangements.

3 BE CAREFUL WITH JOBS

If you take a casual job, babysitting or cleaning, or something similar for pocket money, try to make sure that your parents go with you in the first instance to make sure that everything is in order.

If you are babysitting, and someone comes

to the door *do not* let them in, and do not tell them that you are alone. Telephone the parents' contact number and tell them about it.

If you are doing a paper round and someone offers you a lift (especially if it is raining) you must say **no**! and move on quickly.

4 EMERGENCY NUMBERS

Wherever you are you should always make sure that you have someone to contact or a number to call in an emergency.

4 DON'T KEEP A BAD SECRET!

If a grown-up touches or kisses you, and tries to tell you that this is your secret, this is a *bad secret*, and you should tell your parents straight away.

You probably like kisses and cuddles from your parents, but because your body is your own, you are still free to choose to refuse them from anyone, especially anyone who tells you that the touching must be a secret.

5 YOU DON'T HAVE TO BE RUDE TO SAY NO

If you are approached by someone asking you to go with them or to do something that you feel is wrong, you can politely but firmly refuse, or even pretend not to have heard them. You should try to find a responsible person, like a teacher or a policeman, and tell them. If you cannot find someone like this, try and find a couple or a lady to tell (a shopkeeper, for example).

6 BULLIES

Just because you are learning Karate this does not mean that you have to fight everyone. Bullies are usually cowards, and inadequate people. Very often they will back off if their demands are refused firmly and loudly, and they are left in no doubt that an adult will be told of their behaviour.

Remember that your safety is worth more than your bike or other possessions! Your parents would rather have you home safely without them than in a mess. Try and remember details of what the bully looked like, and what he or she was wearing.

Glossary

Age-uke: Upward Block

Bu: Martial/Warlike
Budo: Martial Ways
Bunkai: Kata applications
Bushi: Warrior
Bushido: The Warrior's Way (Code)

Choku-zuki: Straight Punch
Chudan: Middle Level

Dachi: Stance
Dan: Step (Black-belt Grade)
Do: Way (of)
Dojo: Place where the "Way" is practised

Empi/Enpi: Elbow
Empi/Enpi: Flying Swallow (Name of Kata)
Empi/Enpi-uchi: Elbow Strike

Fudo-dachi: Immovable Stance (also called "Sochin-Dachi")
Fumikomi: Stamping Kick

Gedan: Lower Level
Gedan-barai: Downward Sweeping Block
Geri: Kick
Gi: Training Suit
Go: Five
Go: Hard
Gohon-kumite: Five-step Sparring
Gyaku-zuki: Reverse Punch

Hai: Yes
Hajime!: Begin!
Haito: Ridge Hand
Hansoku: Foul
Hantei: Decision (by Referee)
Hara: Belly (Spiritual Centre)
Heisoku-dachi: Informal Attention Stance
Hidari: Left

Ichi: One (number)
Ippon: One
Ippon: One point

Jodan: Upper Level
Ju: Soft, Pliable
Ju: Ten
Ju-dachi: Free Stance
Ju-kumite: Free-Sparring
Jutsu: Art

-ka: Practitioner (as in Karate-ka)
Kakato: Heel
Kamaite!: Action! (Command)
Kara: Chinese
Kara: Empty
Kata: Formal sequence of techniques
Ke-age: Upward Snapping
Kekomi: Thrusting
Ken: Fist
Ki: Inner Power, Spirit
Kiai: Shout
Kiba-dachi: Straddle-Leg Stance
Kihon: Basic
Kihon-ippon-kumite: Basic One-Step Sparring
Kime: Focus
Kokutsu-dachi: Back Stance
Kun: Motto, Promise
Kyu: Boy, Grade (below Black-Belt)

Ma-ai: Correct Distance
Mae: Front
Mae-geri: Front Kick
Mawashi-geri: Roundhouse Kick
Mawatte: Turn
Migi: Right
Mikazuki-geri: Crescent Kick

Neko-ashi-dachi: Cat Foot Stance
Nukite: Spear Hand

Obi: Belt
Oi-zuki: Lunge Punch

Rei: Bow

Samurai: Warrior
Sanbon-zuki: Three Punches
Sempai: Senior
Sensei: Teacher
Shizentai: Natural Stance
Shuto: Knife Hand
Soto ude-uke: Forearm Block from outside

Te: Hand
Teisho: Palm Heel
Tetsui: Bottom Fist

Uchi: Strike
Uchi: Inside
Uchi ude-uke: Forearm Block from inside
Uke: Block
Ura: Back
Uraken: Backfist
Ushiro: Rear/Backward
Ushiro-geri: Back Kick

Waza: Technique, Skill
Waza-ari: Near Point

Yakusoku: Pre-arranged
Yame!: Stop!
Yoi!: Ready!
Yoko: Side
Yoko-geri: Side Kick

Zanshin: Awareness
Zen: Buddhist Philosophy
Zenkutsu-dachi: Front Stance
Zuki: Punch

Numbers

Ichi: One
Ni: Two
San: Three
Shi: Four
Go: Five
Rokyu: Six
Shichi: Seven
Hachi: Eight
Ku: Nine
Ju: Ten